LEADERS IN MY COMMUNITY

I WANT TO BE A SENATOR

by Jennifer Boothroyd

Consultant: Beth Gambro
Reading Specialist, Yorkville, Illinois

Minneapolis, Minnesota

Teaching Tips

Before Reading

- Look at the cover of the book. Discuss the picture and the title.

- Ask readers to brainstorm a list of what they already know about senators. What can they expect to see in the book?

- Go on a picture walk, looking through the pictures to discuss vocabulary and make predictions about the text.

During Reading

- Read for purpose. Encourage readers to think about the state they live in as they are reading.

- Ask readers to look for the details of the book. What are they learning about the job of senators?

- If readers encounter an unknown word, ask them to look at the sounds in the word. Then, ask them to look at the rest of the page. Are there any clues to help them understand?

After Reading

- Encourage readers to pick a buddy and reread the book together.

- Ask readers to name two things a senator does. Find the pages that tell about these things.

- Ask readers to write or draw something they learned about being a senator.

Credits:
Cover and title page, © AndruGoldman/iStock, © TimeImage Production/Shutterstock; 3, © Marti Bug Catcher/Shutterstock; 5, © AndruGoldman/iStock and © diignat/Shutterstock; 6–7, © adamkaz/iStock; 8–9, © Picturellarious/Adobe Stock; 10–11, © Sipa USA/Alamy; 13, © dpa picture alliance/Alamy; 14–15, © Richard Ellis/Alamy; 17, © Mangostar/Shutterstock; 18–19, © CrackerClips Stock Media/Shutterstock; 21, © Prostock-studio/Shutterstock; 22T, © PeopleImages.com - Yuri A/Shutterstock; 22M, © Littlekidmoment/Shutterstock; 22B, © New Africa/Adobe Stock; 23TL, © Pixel-Shot/Adobe Stock; 23TM, © oliverdelahaye/Shutterstock; 23TR, © Xinhua / Alamy; 23BL, © Denys Holovatiuk/Adobe Stock; 23BR, © SeventyFour/Shutterstock.

STATEMENT ON USAGE OF GENERATIVE ARTIFICIAL INTELLIGENCE
Bearport Publishing remains committed to publishing high-quality nonfiction books. Therefore, we restrict the use of generative AI to ensure accuracy of all text and visual components pertaining to a book's subject. See BearportPublishing.com for details.

Library of Congress Cataloging-in-Publication Data is available at www.loc.gov or upon request from the publisher.

ISBN: 979-8-88916-268-1 (hardcover)
ISBN: 979-8-88916-273-5 (paperback)
ISBN: 979-8-88916-277-3 (ebook)

Copyright © 2024 Bearport Publishing Company. All rights reserved. No part of this publication may be reproduced in whole or in part, stored in any retrieval system, or transmitted in any form or by any means, electronic, mechanical, photocopying, recording, or otherwise, without written permission from the publisher.

For more information, write to Bearport Publishing, 5357 Penn Avenue South, Minneapolis, MN 55419.

Contents

I Want to Lead 4

Be a Leader Now 22

Glossary 23

Index 24

Read More 24

Learn More Online......................... 24

About the Author 24

I Want to Lead

The United States has rules called **laws**.

Where do these laws come from?

Senators make them.

I want to be a senator!

Every **state** has two U.S. senators.

People from the state **vote** for who they want.

Senators have their jobs for six years.

Senators work for everyone in their state.

But they do not stay in their state to work.

They go to Washington, D.C.

There, all the senators from the United States come together.

These 100 people make rules for everyone in the **country**.

Senators also work with people from the House of **Representatives**.

These people come from different states, too.

They also help make laws!

Say representatives like *rep*-ri-ZEN-tuh-tivz

Senators go to their states often.

That way, they can hear about what people there want.

They learn ways to make the country better.

Sometimes, senators from different states want the same thing.

They work together to make laws.

Some laws keep people safe.

Others are about treating all people fairly.

Many laws keep the air and water clean.

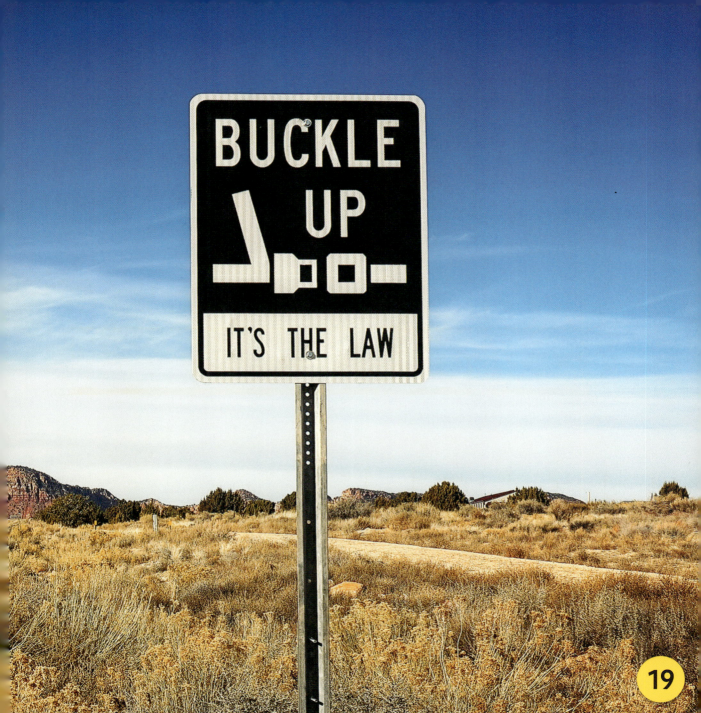

Being a senator is a big job.

Laws need to help everyone.

But I think I could do it!

Be a Leader Now

There are many ways you can be a leader before you become a senator.

Listen to your friends. Help them when they need a hand.

Write a letter or an email to your senators. Share your ideas about helping the country.

Think about the rules at school. What new rule would make school better? Bring your ideas to your teacher.

Glossary

country an area of land that has borders and rules for all the people there

laws rules that people must follow

representatives people who speak for a larger group

state an area of land with its own rules that is inside a country

vote to make a choice about someone or something

Index

fair 18
law 4, 12, 16, 18, 20
representatives 12
safe 18
state 4, 7–8, 11, 16
vote 7
Washington, D.C. 8

Read More

Gaston, Stephanie. *Senator (The Job of a Civic Leader).* Coral Springs, FL: Seahorse Publishing, 2023.

Schuh, Mari C. *The Senate (Our Government).* Minneapolis: Bellwether Media, 2021.

Learn More Online

1. Go to **www.factsurfer.com** or scan the QR code below.
2. Enter **"To Be Senator"** into the search box.
3. Click on the cover of this book to see a list of websites.

About the Author

Jenny Boothroyd has been to the Capitol building in Washington, D.C. One day she hopes to see the room where the senators meet.